T0266364

ANIMAL DAYS

ANIMAL DAYS

Joshua Beckman

WAVE BOOKS / SEATTLE AND NEW YORK

Published by Wave Books

www.wavepoetry.com

Copyright © 2021 by Joshua Beckman

All rights reserved

Wave Books titles are distributed to the trade by

Consortium Book Sales and Distribution

Phone: 800-283-3572 / SAN 631-760X

Library of Congress Cataloging-in-Publication Data

Names: Beckman, Joshua, 1971– author.

Title: Animal days / Joshua Beckman.

Description: Seattle : Wave Books, 2021.

Identifiers: LCCN 2020015675 | ISBN 9781950268108 (hardcover)

ISBN 9781950268092 (paperback)

Subjects: LCGFT: Poetry.

Classification: LCC PS3552.E2839 A85 2021 | DDC 811/.54—dc23

LC record available at https://lccn.loc.gov/2020015675

Designed by Crisis

Printed in the United States of America

9 8 7 6 5 4 3 2 1

First Edition

Wave Books 089

Thanks to my friends, family, and everyone at Wave for
their support. And thank you to the Lannan Foundation.

IT SEEMED TOO MUCH

it seemed
too much
   —the
clacking +
griping, the going
 back + forth
it's not him
nor is it anything
else—
    I capture my
fears in a cup
like a sample
and yell out

   the pursing
  and bursting
  of cells
  blood
  in the skin
  in the face
  blood exploding
   inside us
   like that

———

chest
filled out
with toxic air
and
dogged
by sensible
exclamation
I look up
witness around me
the careening sparks
of private dissent
and just
describe it or something

that plastic
ritual of under-
standing
and being here
resulting in shame

———

curt stones
stomach pain
body pain — cell
+ task
I feel
that ruinous gutter
rasping

landing
punch-like
between the mouth
and the pubis or
on this day I
sleep — the
hot excrement
making itself
within me
from soup

———

Dog
children
splashing with air
in their mouths
spitting grotesque
sounds

a waiting
waxy thing
sat in its
own bladder

spastic crabs
of mouth
+ done
veins + blood

mute
    night scum

    then back
    to the city
  w/ a hole
  in my tongue

—

finger-sized shot
stingy and bitter not
up in the hills
breathing

      cocked shadows
of quizzical soot
      a fearful
crying zeppelin for
a mind and filling
myself with nothing
relax
    now it's basically
nighttime, the grey clouds
      soon won't even
seem to be there
        dripping
squash of rained upon building
  rained upon
building

cupping strange light
    & "Shakespearean Tears"
    growing fern-like
    in the railroad's dell
    flashing spit
    of concrete bridge

                    (lightning)

            rows of house-sized masses

                    (lightning)

            tombs of dirt, piles, a
            kind of nothing-dumpsters

                    (lightning)

    tent pulled rope
    up to a tree
    the sun it shines
    the air with white

    while I
    like an enormous
    pillow of muck
    on the other hand
    seem to be moving
    all the time

                    10:33
                        porch

                    bridge
                            jell

                    plastic sky-
        like slabs

                    ———

chrome soup fog
and hash muck
coating the
notebook's flat side
Day 2 it says
but that was weeks ago
up up with
the air a little bird
is taken
and I think

              puff
              trash
              breeze
              light
              little bird

                              (Goodbye Friend)

LITTLE PRICKLY COMING OF STORM

*

an
afternoon
dissolves

and
in
the sun
we see
an egret
officially
injuncting

as it pokes
into the fleshy
fish with its
beak and has it
speared there

then
throws back
its head
so the creature
goes perfectly
vertically up

and in a straight line
comes all the way
back down
right into
its mouth

day in day
out there on logs
and such

people coming down
through the bushes
wearing hats

with similar
fantastical
moments emblazoned
in silhouette

but just consider
the living creature
who does something
like that

the terrible
crushing of bones
and eating

**

I, myself
            earliest
    and first
            displaced into a
satchel-shaped
            silhouette
    of two fish
        bumping chest—
    and everyone thought,
        smiling

Second,
    same thing
            and so on

weightless
    obliviation
            of it never
        ending

    I remember as
waves in circles
    pools and spirals
            round a pole

                    oyster
                shell dust
                in the dirt
                and in the air

          a sheet
        of it
        held
        constellation-like
              in the back yard
        responding
                to wind

          clothespins for
          fingers

                  houses
          blown down the road
                through the town

                  like a toy
        the way you can see
      all parts of
                it—and
        when you turn
              it over
          a vase and mirror
                    glazed
            finish
            on

                        ***

sink caves of
stain — classic
            misty
                and
        angel
            in day
        visits
            cave

    from
      cave
        too
      we
        see

    the water parting
    the sky parting
    the clouds

buzzard-
        headed
    nicked and placid

I sensed in just hearing it a kind of

        (someone had been there)

                    and when I tapped
            on the little mouthpiece
        its plastic
            tack and its

                    electric trill
        rightened up
            a moment
                and settled
                    back

                    and I tapped it again
                    and it did it again

                            shimmering
                            stag bells
                            in glass
                            casque

        donor crows
            quacking + spazzing

My god – I had no idea what you've been saying all
this time – in another hour, little clips of light,
broad swaths of greying sky – from my tongue to
everywhere (mountains and planets)

So I put it back up to my ear – deafening opaque noes
smooshed up against the glass it would be embarrassing
if I wasn't trying so hard

                    flat—grass stained
                or slayed treeline
                        from train—

            a metal tin
                of caves and glass tables

the project
of my every word tinking
and tapping that glass

cold stone sandals
terrible on the back

massive
and foreboding

****

so undone

pulsing pools
light each
cauliflower lamb
and licking
me shyly
on the calves

my meat and
my muscle
vanished in an
odd showing off
plucked and itchy

hairs getting pulled out
tin crosses in

the ceiling—
know/half
known or so

a kind of
  newly magical
    tactic

explosive coasting tones

curious
    not to be seen
out of them—

fallen now—bone—
        like muscle
            clutching my
      temples forcefully
racked against a tree

  one half-cracked head
  one falling out into the

  (seeming
  to dance around
    thoughtless)

    then flags—stacked
in the path behind here

smelling half oyster
half wax—smelling
everything with
this nose

*****

I broadcast
now in spats
+ tugs

(weather-like)

how foggy it is
this floating

I could just say
it was raining

now it is night

I didn't make
it out of the house

a lion seems
jammed
between a car
and a dumpster

plastic lights
   in high
  passive
     flap

 curtains
   broken
       wag

leaking
  tintinnabulum

             found
             loved
             needed

  then
    let to
      go out
    underneath
    a wash ageless
  misjunct of fear
       and loss—

   seen you crowd
       in an evil ball
  almost yourself

   grabbing in trials
 too drawn from the
    happy hunt –

tragic hacking into
walls—classic passing
        and even feeling
    for it—

    aphids munching
        and munching
        on house-
        plants

            sanded
        bauble-sized
    colorless
        in the sunshine
        and in the night

            so half seeings
            pourn out half

            ******

    left his
spiritual quest
        to someone else

    countrysides of pine

fragrant sun
            angular shade

span of comers
day of hours
month of day etc.

while back in the café
now like a cone of sugar
he sat

and outside cold frozen noses
were dripping drops of blood
from boys with pupped out tongues

Soon the sterile
ponds of ice
will make fragrant bits of pine expire

flesh and clove
of knuckle froze

pours and spouts
smashed they shatter
crushed they hold
their shattered form

and when he steps out into it, that's how
he seems, inside some wretched civic square
of squat and cry,

a little deer
prancing in the fallen pines
eating butterflies

living on nothing, as they say
and showing nothing's particular nimbleness

and so wandering around and rebuked
by the very vocabulary of his scheming
he dragged with effort
his body along the pavement
knocking and crashing to the
delight of all but the ones
he crushed

****

Sitting down outside the temple
my gelatinous ass cooled
by the stone shelf, I felt
each articulate pop
of sand-sized hail
projecting water's glassy substance
in frozen seeds

but I was retching and farting and messing the whole
thing up, when a lovely skinny man like a fox
came over and started to sniff

I cracked myself
upon the surface
in anger
and shattered
and there

a plate of ice formed
    like a cavity
        of the moon
            filled in

        a frozen glassy earth
                on which to fall

            life of bone bone life
            of bone – life of bone
            bone life of bone –

despairs of the given up form he thought
and bladelike down the hill an easy and
suffering cry tobogganed on

            it's winter once
                again and up he leaned

                    a heavy sort of stoic
    want glazed his static face

                _____

                so there I sat
                on the stone shelf

            tugging at my other bare foot

        hasty and engaged
                            I was
            tired

24

THE GLACIAL TRIP

so beeps
        the flattened
disheveled mind
            sternly pressed

        the winter it is
        winter or the winter
        it is coming

            I see the arcs and lines
        of metal round some baby tree
            and on my stoop
        in bars and gates
before it snows
            the sun is out

                —

        blood shed skin
    and the hair
            that filled my pocket
and the fat that made
        my mind a thing

scratch those
factual distractions
into me—your head like
a dog's on mine lay
all the way down

first cold
morning dreams
then sweat
then freeze

—

premonitions useless
I got into bed
with my feet sticking out

the phone was
on the hump of a book

there was
no one around,
and it was quiet

I stole to my own
cross ways
like I was reading something,
needing to read it again
and again

I have a sentence
like that
stuck up my ass
and wiggling
like a fish

I turn
the page
and something
else might happen

"under this puck of sun
the first city was built"

He said it in a kind of angry
way – my arms wrapped around the
morning like it was a tree and I was
wrapped around it and (time passing)
my skull on my head like I usually wear it

—

October over
ripened plastic object
moonward crying touches
of breath

and branches picked
on evening meander

only cats think
of bringing everything round
purring over everything
 mooing on call to offer
blissful elevating ritual
 pile of eaten mush

 eclipsing proof of endless
material olive-colored top of
boulder etched realistically
 plain, our eden-minded others
plastered ohs over beaded ear
 ecstatically maudlin

on the counter cuz the place was
 filling up / touching around my body
to see what was tender bruised then
 ripped out over cracked rabble of
built engine cracked egg on table

—

dumps + wagons

raining down
of plastic sound
        pelting rooftop

distracting
at first then just
boring + tragic

you who have
from my
with me

collapsed
illusion in
metallic sphere

after which
looking into it
and thinking
probably too long

I lie here now
in back defying
mattress on floor
in back defying
posture to stay warm

I have been
for at least
an hour now
rubbing my feet
together

—

2nd half
of the letter
to everyone
cat is alive, cat is dead
flakey spangled shiny
belt of human in the scene

rock jaw plunked
in middle of desert
and waiting

small flake of fathomed feelings

tin human creations

stick-high grass
from part the mucky river
styled by a kind of awareness

living sign of sage a green and grey
terrible nasty decorative human
put in my place by you

stunned again by the dumb cup
I filled it up, that's what
you said I'd do

—

Meaningless
         bunches of sweat
   pooled in the city's
         dry eye as salt
terra-cotta crystal
         and match

      formless navies of
   cloud barreling down

      hate I see and
      thinking hate I know

rock salt flat
   classic signs I

         with massive
            god's head on my belly

   I with great mean bear
   on my belly too

         pull my pants all
   the way up, my

         pissing done and left
   my shirt in a pile

   what strange names are
   these are they what
      embodied mes and Is

then ghostly my shirt
filled with air
and rose up full,
waist high

—

pissy animals
nasty and surly
climbing out window
and into the world

I watch from my seat
pawing and waving

until someone
puts something
in front of me to drink
and I drink

How are you they
asked again today

I'm suspended like
a little pill
in a juicy juicy body

But what kind of answer is that

—

muscled hands
　　and toothless showers
　　　　crazy graphic crying
　　　　and kissing

　　　(massive sludgies)

　　　　　and the wall
　　left there in all its
　　　　archaeological splendor

　walked with your mom
　walked with the people you cared for

　　splashing end of DC scene
　　　cracked beneath
　　　　the water

　　　　jaws + ears

—

　　　Something terrible
　　　　and sanguine
　writ into
　　　the plan

I can't
really even believe
where I am –

plant note
raw + soaked

whatever strange
knockings around there are
I hear them

3am
and from the moonlit street
a resonating sound
bellied out

not that I was
or should have been
to sleep already

but those nail-footed
rat creatures
got me here

standing at the window
hands in my hair

—

The conduct
        of life the
                young and the evil
    all came over same
                night unannounced

                crab-like
    flashings
                and pickings

    candles
        flickering
    still in apartment

    quiet
      looking down
        from the window
                onto layers of junk
        forming there
in absolutes

        pocked and scruffed
          in an organic and almost
            geological way compelling
                    after standing
            there a minute
                I opened
                the door

                —

                    glass buttons
        + shards—not
                    people—3rd
        stroke of it
                    it's gone away
        it stayed away
                    not smiling
        not being there
                    with them
            just lope
    of moving pulse
        inside my body
    forming
        outside my
            body too

            architecture's
                my hobby now
                and rodent-like
        I run around
    through open
        doors into
        warm cozy
        passageways
            gutter + pipe

                    —

                    38

I prepared this story
called <u>The Glacial</u>
<u>Trip</u> in which
gathering stuff at
the dock + waiting
to hitch a ride back
into town

+

back into town
covered over
with ecstatic parody
of cloth—buttons
on it—of tin
but they didn't
hurt they felt mostly
like a cold natural
surface pressing
comfortably against
the skin

palmy sleeping
afternoon +
lung breathing +
warm human eyes
+ deck-trayed backs of cow
in their mouths

it was feast-like
and my head hanging
out the window just

saw what was
      there out the
         window—to be seen
            weeds
      growing
and a perpetuate
         curiosity just
            had me cutting
         them down, trimming
               them—but either
         way there they were
      growing in ivy-like
masses + I'm sure

      rags hanging from the
               fence bottom to
         distract the order

      this is what I mean
         when I say flags
strips or squares of cloth
         hung out in the
               air + flapping
                  around

                        —

I answer again
   to the dumb question

                    muscles felt
                    visions flexed

and with just a little
        hair in my eye I became
    distracted I cried

        from the couch
    to the rest of the world
            my displeasures
                        extend

                people scattered epistolarily
                with my hand

        rain showers
        and time seen through
        the constant recurrence of night

                            41

DRAWING X'S ON THE TABLE

static
    pulsing
        stacks
and dancing selves

perhaps I waited here
    inside this suit for you

ugly pumpkin flesh
upsetted now in memory

        songs upsetting myths
and singing so
        inside you now
            it bubbles out

*

B----

    loved
in another
    land or so
        him half knotted
up in himself

45

sifts a puffing air
out nostrils
          mine and his

      this ecstatic and barely
barely imaginable bubble

                              in which
                    I am now
                              protected

          slow decaying dirtyish self
          my wants grew – I clanked them
          on the wooden bar on the glass too

      and these bashings and these kickings
knock out another tooth

                    *

          little flat
leaf lay down
      from tree
      on head
          a brushed
          bit scrubbed
                    off + told
          me its story

others arrive
give pout
stroke face
with one's own
split open
star of
skin and blood

sick wailing
so loud
that getting there
then heaving
shaky and
sad

*

don't know
why it has to
be some thing
anyway – 1st
parasitic classic
like room-light
on body
up
and heaving

teeth scrubbed
termite crushed

wind delayed in other kinds
of stagnant air

gnat crushed
ant crushed
dead wasp speared with
tip of pencil
outlandish
sterile
and mean

*

the spring day as it
did the summer as
it does the fall
now as it will
the winter soon

————

I heard in
the continued
pressing down
of notes
on the piano
as I sat in my
chair with your
book in my lap

thinking
how will I
return this to
you and when

reading it
even as I
got reading
it even as
I write you
this letter

*

sitting here
with some dream
of it California
beach nearby
story
of having
and thinking

Ben about
the dunes
says Oh!

zoo made
cedar pillar
walk and

all the
creatures
on it went
out to
view + touch
the ocean

but Ben
I think
was most
impressed
by the quietness
and me too
as if photographed

the crystal
sand has
stilled +
through this
enormous
cloud of proof
the waking
walkers move

*

musky smells
of man
enwrapping

                smells
                  of sweat

      drifting
          parkward

                            ocean
                                breeze

                  I think
                mash stain meat
              and gripe
                  splattered
              on the
              pharmacy
          wall looking
            like ringlet
                    waves
              or dripping
          mud chills
    inside my muscles too
          piles of
              people
                  junk tears
                    mindless
                              enwitting
                        sniffs
                  and seen

                          *

                          51

crabby
moon clothes
belt +
stockings
today I saw
a critter
with a wallow
like a skunk
his white mane
lit up by
the moon
foxes
proliferating
as in fairy
tales + dreams
spiders too
marvelous +
terrifying insects
riding around
on deer like
vikings

*

squads of
pluck + gong
of drum
passively hostile
efforts of

                    mind
        now
          surging

          else-
      ward

        in ghostly loping
          claim
              that bloody mug

        coursing dustpacks
      and pellets
    fill me up

            and when
                the hands
                    before my
                face part
        I feel
          my cheekbones
      bulge in
        reddish boney
            sphere-like humps
                  + my
          lips in
            smile puck up
        terrifyingly

                          *

pacified almost crushed
I tagged my face to
make that sound
as I was bored
and had begun to feel
            optimistically stylized

                  in form of empty
            cardboard box

      the fruit
        beneath the foot sole

   compounded speck
     of something juicy smooshed

   hoping to account for as much
   of everything as I could but I had
   left out most of what was happening
   choosing instead a kind of
   domestic composition

            you were
               living with me
         we were there
            and in our home
            that's how it happened

      I would sit
         in front of the poem
       or really the poem would

sit there on the table
a cup on it too

*

flick of my
closed eye
        and feel it then
    in lying there

————————

        why do you
puff from anger
            with me

(bird-like in this sense meaning
relating to each other in constant
jerky motions and also flying
in easeful synchronicities too)

            charm soak bloom
            of brothers above
                seeing each other
            from way up high

        leaves spread in nets
                around their trees –

shiners with their nets
        in the cold water

    opening wide
            their arms
        fernlike
            netty too

    starting now
    to feel
            light-headed
            and good

                    *

    signs
    beat
    the sweat
on my head
    bent over my head
    funneling down
    showerless
pooling + dripping

    feeling that same
            hot constant
        encountering
        cold air
    yesterday

all day
            yesterday
today all day
            today

                        *

            warm
                        body
of ate things – causing
            itself to
                sweat and shake
                            tired miles away
            from my bed

                    faces + eyes

                        *

                            pails
                of water
                        + dome-like
            homes for piles
                of frozen dirt

        boarded up windows
    and doors

mud tracks froze
    in the foot
        that made them

    cattail fannings
as do people
        retreating in failing
    or surging light

                            *

ice water
        and little
            bits of leg
    in the bucket

forefoot
    pushed against
        wall of plastic

    hoof scratching
            + knee eaten

        delivered in task I am
            listening

                watching the red light
        fill its curtain
            like a wind

the street lights
glow and spread

us as being here
me as being here

*

breath of day
and souls braided
tight in soft delightful air

spare worries and
blocked-up veins
the costly suctioning out
of blood or pus
the muck of earth
lapsed in collapsing grunts
of laughter

that's the drugs talking
that's the drugs making
you feel that way

nervous frothy
scum of earth-filled air
foaming up
to fill it seemed
wrappers of trash
balanced atop it

look how you do
as the scum jumps your leg
dread little babies
sucking in bubbles

it's coarse and mean I think
to point it out
and evilly weak
to act as it's not there

and passive passive passive
your poem about the air

*

No will to
be good for
anything
I lifted
my arm
+
crashed it
down on
the house
and uncharacteristically
and impossibly
the house
split in half

so now we're
separated by
more than just
ourselves

lashes of
drastic treeline
traps
not good
not melancholy
but sorrowful
and real

each
had come
to be about
a bounding or
pulsing of
body

the foot down
the fist
the tapping hand
the breath
the little impulse too
in rounded
waves
outward

like terrible
stamping child

I seemed
putting on my shoes
in fits of sound
and dust-like specters
having been
fill the air

body

mask

+

hole

*

my occult diary
was boring
angelic rafts and fire pits
tuned to abstract people
I'd hear the buzz
and shock
enough
parades of gruesome
preachings absolutely
unnecessary
as I was still
dealing with the

effects of that
sound when the next
one came

chemistry's
actual bubbling up
chemistry's actual
bubbling up
in waves of
unapproachable
feeling

K's eyes
unapproachably
opaque

then less so as the
ride went on

iris-sized prides of ants and bugs
distracting in practice of moving
around and doing – then next morning
missing them then finding them again
in an apple or part apple left on
the floor

towns in mist winter trees in
mist continuous placation of air
and water lapping ocean-like from
the sky down

63

But still chipped hands become poisoned the
cracks widened were filled with coke dust
blood oozed from them Everything I touched
caused me pain I avoided and neglected I drove
my friends from me In an attack of righteous
indignation and overwhelmed by a furious desire to do
myself injury, I committed suicide by dispatching an
infamous unpardonable letter, casting off my wife and
child forever

                    Strindberg

              what a bastard

          Stories of the Poisoned Biography

              isolated in
                       strange
            excess of
                      effort
            heard

          *

each thousandth
    layer of piss
+ sweat
    laid down
+ coated

in nasty constants
never cleaned

so the perfume
as it were
of everybody

holding
        nose and
            lashing out

a fall
and other
        person
poking double-
fingered faces
        + mouths

children
        pour
        out drying
rings
    of clay

seem hard
        + done

clay sense
        of people
            piss and mud
    fumes from body

entombed—fumes
from people
into you

*

fabulous
        palettes
                of actual
ash + moss
red in berry
        human faced

racing gasps
        of dead tree
    wet seeming
moss-coated
            + poking
                        into air

I have sent you home in the
terrible world where you live

        campground
        precinct
        bug

*

oils
+ fragrance
of self-
carved
moon
in thigh
massaging + rubbing
the muscles
like that

veins
touched
full of blood
a kind of
hosting

gross + total

*

lead wire tombs
made and cast

moist slips of paper rubbed
on flesh
and feeling
muscle

hard cone of sweat
　smell dried and salt
lit room lit room
up sour

　　plaster masks
and deep reclining lines
　of time
　　things being noted
upon it
　　even read
　　　and what you
　　say to me now about this
　　　I remember

　　　　elsewhere
　　released from the mold
　　　I saw its form

　　and tagged with distracting
　signs, the pain in my leg
　　where its pulse was released

　　　　　*

　　　　describing
　　　　　the countryside
　　　　I think in

ODE TO THE PICTURE
OF HEALTH AND VITALITY

glorious bridges

through space : through starlight

into one's own principles
into one's own thoughts

as for leaving
I was just slow
as I was
with everything else

spheres
like
homes , he said

neoclassical dystopian and
spheres like homes

constellated
and lacquer casts
made for describing

waited there, Dec 5,

2015

AUGUST

I most like
    the order of statues
        begin to weed
            the marble weeds

      I flapped
        (flapflap)
        sweat drops
and everything
    the fan at myself

      the wood is fat
      with water and heat

  it's bowing the door
    so it never closes

      …

      crowny sounds
  and volcanic warmth
      spread out in pulses

ashen creatures
flora too

dry buzzing lights
go by now in form of fly

sharing the spirit
in person
moths flap
and touch me also

...

loveheads bobbing
along the walkway
ears full

crow with
half-open mouth
beak still on
powerlines
soundless

...

the smoke's already
come for our lungs

and selves still plate-like
seem unstuck

...

summer's seams
and summer's net in webbings

pigeons peck
at what green that's left

in hay-like grasses
gold and dead

...

fog-eyed
in nighttime

actual acts
of fear I spun
and stood

ending in the evening
open eyes aflood

...

    here I keep
  even on cold days
     the windows open

           (buses & cars)

...

No morning woke
No yowling cat

the city's device decries

while on the bus
such slight and finest
toilettes are made

a little spit of paper
tacked to the front door

...

relieved
of senses
by the sky,
soft cold pulls
and giant sighs

this sharp
ting of the eye
where the smoke
comes in

...

sick seeming fever
and somehow ate
half a pound
of sugar

home two days
cleaned and ordered

cats back and forth
across the carpeted floor

heat in its strange process
pours into my heavy chest

cottaged small and harmless
as we are, hoarse

                    the throat,
                        and hoarse
                    this gravelly part
                of my equipment
                            says hello

                            ...

                            smoke fog
                    fixed itself
                on the region

            ridge and flat
                dry grass lots
                warehouse and dune

                    bare trees
                on beach the
                    orange sun

                            ...

                    cut down half
                        of chill

                            brought up as bugs
                    the pounding and pulsing

...

Light from the drone's eye
flashes in the heavens again
and seizes on the wheels of a train

       drags and jams
         of moment wedged
            a dent, a daily leveling

I imagine you approach
through the approaching smoke

a thin line
     of anger and fright
          run through it

...

           you see
        the tiredness
          inside someone
        as they sleep

        you see
     a path around
       the balls and bits
            of bread

crows
       retreating
and

a light grey
   shades the city

       . . .

September 1

flailing around

September 2

I could see who was alive
now and who died

I could see now
who was dead

who was alive

ANIMAL DAYS

I had just a minute left
         and with it stood

   harmless blowing out
of waxy candle

      its smell and dark

      ...

all the way now
    I think of you

how do you stop and look in their eyes

how do you get on the ground
    to be next to them

      ...

     you were turning the page
     and saying something like

this person was wild and special
or this person was particularly kind

...

light cold
pulses around
my body

my bed wobbles
till it's still

in the night woods
man's curious remains
turn circular round
each thought and theorem

...

and from this
painted cinematic half-dream
I felt my energy drain

day's over
and I do flood
with sadness

yet there it is:

Night's long guardings
graceful and angular
while
raw flotsam
arcing and spinning
in the fire
turns to ash

...

broad
and stoned
and gone before
the bird's whoo
on its pallet
of rock
ended

I too am singing
awkwardly to myself
is it fear?

they are always saying it is fear
but I suspect a kind of
dumbness lapping and growling
insensitively within me

caused it first myself
then now responding to
its empty echo

I carry on with a thud
a thud thud, a thud thud thud
  a thud thud thud
  a thud thud thud

...

The winter sand in pits and piles
owls and rodents, craws unstuck
and rabbits hop around in moonlight

awaiting some friend's golden form
I look out into it and find firstly
stars and time then night surrounding

its matter still dark, its cautions
its hemorrhaging grass and acting coarse

its chills and aches made oceans
and with nearly the same it dried them
right up

...

I pulled over
  to see every hill

light down
    at the base
        of the mountain

dead cars bright
  projections of themselves
    scattered in a lot

          ...

wind poem one dragged out of me
light color red dragged out of me
water come out of me left dry
a wind blows the page as I write

          ...

I received three letters today

I saw on the warming surface some specks
dance around and catch fire and after that
the air expand

I peeled an orange
because my throat was dry

I read "How useless is the human
turning fresh water to salt"

rubbed down rocks and pasted stains
onto otherwise empty sheets of paper

...

the sky came up
through the grass this morning
seeping out of the ground

and the cautious light alights
and the body's sign's described

I am cooled and my hopes are cooled

all day they say a thousand years
and smile

a million years and smile and smile

a thousand million years

...

     Moon craters
and their quartz-filled lines of light

hog-like creatures
    ripping up the grass

healthy young souls,
their spirits intact, I think
lying in the breeze with the half-open door
aluminum and hot, hopes and ideas
again as always, but still

    the earth recast its
  healing glow
    brightened
        and painful

        ...

    Noon calls morning
        and the face of
      moon in rock

        I spit
          w/ a kind of
     relaxed spasm
        into the air

     body's fears shown
      in phlegm

and the little creatures scamper
        harmless through
        the garden
        or so it seems

just a rooting around
for their food and
some re-animation
of topsoiled dirt

...

a smell comes up
        to the human nose
sweet and musky
        and the spot where
I have sat each day
sipping my coffee
        seems foreign
                and earthy

                as bark where
        it is burnt or straw
releasing its sign
        to the world a decay

        and I crawl as my
                worm spirit shows
        through the turned dirt
                        for my lighter

        poisoned sores exposed
                I give it blood

let's call this

ANIMAL DAYS

where the soft bee pokes
   its one appendage

and the butterfly yielding waits

...

               a radiant glimmer
  I once saw in eye
                I once felt in tongue
   how stupid wet and soft
                they're seeming now

  candid is the flesh
and strange the jaw
            its masticating of everything

  how silly
      its vigilance seems
as the beetle crosses
   back and forth

               and the spider
      makes its little net
   to catch its moving food

diagnostic articulations of self
        all around and being clouded
    with weakness, still attempts
            even so

                a hundred copper pins shake
                with the changes of weather
                    or weather's coming on
            in unnoticeable glows and pulls

            and the problem
                it's strange to say
                is not the being ash
                or the terrible particlization
        so much as the lack
                inside the box
            of anything
                to blow you away

Joshua Beckman was born in New Haven,
Connecticut. His books include *The Lives of
the Poems* and *Three Talks*, *The Inside of an
Apple*, *Take It*, *Shake*, and *Your Time Has Come*.

WAVE BOOKS 089

ISBN 978-1-950268-09-2 $18.00

9 781950 268092